Two Minute SQL - Vol. 1

Brought to you by the staff at SQLServerCentral.com

Thanks to the following for contributing questions:
David Benoit
Kay-Ole Behrmann
Darwin Hatheway
Keith Henry
James Travis

Central Publishing Group
P.O. Box 9510
Fleming Island, FL 32006

Forward

Why Two Minute Questions?

When I was a kid, I used to order these Scholastic mysteries from the school. They were these little, thin paperbacks, like 50-60 or so pages, much like what you're holding now, that had a short mystery written on a page. Usually they consisted of some story and then a question. How did someone get killed? Where did the murder weapon go? Something like that. You then turned the page to find out the answer after thinking about it for a minute.

That's what we're trying to build here, but instead of some mystery, it's a quiz type format of SQL Server questions and answers, culled from the annals of our very popular Question Of The Day on the SQLServerCentral.com website. These are a collection of questions from the past that we put together to help you study for an exam, learn a bit more about SQL Server, pass the time, etc. But they're mostly collected for…

The INTERVIEW.

You're looking for a new job, you've posted your resume, worked on cover letters, and finally landed an interview. Now you want to be sure that you look your best; that you can answer what's thrown at you.

I can't promise that anyone will ask you any of these questions, but you never know. Maybe some managers that are interviewing will grab a copy of the book and start asking questions out of it. But it will help you prepare, give you some hands on experience, challenge you in a variety of ways about the different aspects of SQL Server. Some of the questions are arcane, some very common, but you'll learn something and the wide range of questions will help you get your mind agile and ready for some quick thinking.

So read on, in order, randomly, just start going through them, but do yourself a favor and think about each before turning the page. Challenge yourself and see how well you do.

Thanks for your support and be sure to visit us online.

Steve Jones
SQLServerCentral.com

Question 1 - Administration

Which recovery model would have the largest transaction log backups?

Choose one of the answers below:

1. Simple
2. Full
3. Bulk-logged
4. None of the above

Answer:

3. Bulk-logged

While using the bulk-logged recovery model will keep your transaction logs smaller, your transaction log backups will be larger. This is because each extent that has changed is tracked. When it does change the entire extent is wrapped into the transaction log backup. In Simple recovery model, transaction log backups are not possible and in the Full recovery model, all the transactions are kept.

Question 2 - Administration

How do you make SQL Server 2000 listen on multiple ports?

Choose one of the answers below:

1. Edit the Protocol item of the HKEY_LOCAL_MACHINE\SOFTWARE\Microsoft\MSSQLServer\Client\SuperSocketNetLib key in the registry.
2. Go to Client Network Utilities and select TCP/IP and Properties. Type the ports, separated by spaces and apply the settings. Stop and start SQL Server.
3. Go to Client Network Utilities and select TCP/IP and Properties. Type the ports, separated by commas and apply the settings. Stop and start SQL Server.
4. Go to Server Network Utilities and select TCP/IP and Properties. Type the ports, separated by commas and apply the settings. Stop and start SQL Server.
5. Go to Server Network Utilities and select TCP/IP and Properties. Type the ports, separated by spaces and apply the settings. Stop and start SQL Server.

Answer:

4. Go to Server Network Utilities and select TCP/IP and Properties. Type the ports, separated by commas and apply the settings. Stop and start SQL Server.

You can change the port that SQL Server uses in Server Network Utilties. Select TCP/IP then click Properties. Type the new port or ports (separated by commas) and click apply. Exit the application by clicking OK then stop and start SQL Server to apply the new settings.

See INF: How to Set Up SQL Server 2000 to Listen on Multiple Static TCP Ports

Question 3 - Administration

You are a SQL Server 2000 Administrator. The SQL Server is in a domain called ATLDOM and contains a database called HRData. John is an human resource (HR) representative who uses the database to pull employee salary data for employees. You create a login named ATLDOM\John and manually configure the permissions for her to read selective data from the database.
John then goes on a leave of absense and must not have access to the data for 2 months until he arrives back. When he returns he must easily have access to all the data he had before.
Which Transact-SQL statement should you execute to remove John's server access temporarily?

Choose one of the answers below:

1. EXEC sp_revokedbaccess 'ATLDOM\John'
2. EXEC sp_denylogin 'ATLDOM\John'
3. EXEC sp_droplogin 'ATLDOM\John'
4. EXEC sp_dropuser 'ATLDOM\John'
5. REVOKE ALL TO HRData FROM 'ATLDOM\John'

Answer:

2\. EXEC sp_denylogin 'ATLDOM\John'

By denying him access to the server using the sp_denylogin stored procedure, you ensure that you can quickly reverse the action at a later time. By removing his login altogether, you'll have to explore what permissions he had upon his return and could take much longer.

See sp_denylogin.

Question 4 - Administration

How do you increase the number of SQL Server 2000 error logs that are kept on a SQL Server?

Choose one of the answers below:

1. Right-click on SQL Server Logs in Enterprise Manager and click Configure. Increment the Maximum Number of Logs setting.
2. Modify the MaxLogs item in the HKEY_LOCAL_MACHINE\SOFTWARE\Microsoft\MSSQLServer\MSSQLServer registry key to the new setting.
3. Modify the MaxLogs item in the HKEY_CURRENT_USER\SOFTWARE\Microsoft\MSSQLServer\MSSQLServer registry key to the new setting.
4. Modify the NumErrorLogs item in the HKEY_LOCAL_MACHINE\SOFTWARE\Microsoft\Microsoft SQL Server\MSSQLServer registry key to the new setting.
5. Edit ErrorLog setting in the \Program Files\Microsoft SQL Server\MSSQL\config.ini file.

Answer:

1. Right-click on SQL Server Logs in Enterprise Manager and click Configure. Increment the Maximum Number of Logs setting.

By default, SQL Server stores a very limitted amount of error logs (6 by default). This can pose as a security risk if a hacker cycles the error log to remove traces of his hack. The error log is recycled every time SQL Server is restarted or DBCC ERRORLOG is run. To raise the amount of logs that are kept, right-click on the SQL Server Logs item in Enterprise Manager and click Configure.

See HOW TO: Increase the Number of SQL Server Error Logs.

Question 5 - Administration

How much RAM can SQL Server 2000 Standard Edition see on a Windows 2000 Advanced Server?

Choose one of the answers below:

1. 512 MB
2. 1 GB
3. 2 GB
4. 8 GB
5. 16 GB

Answer:

3. 2 GB

SQL Server 2000 Standard Edition is limitted to 2 GB of memory that it can use. If you want more RAM, then consider upgrading to Enterprise Edition of SQL Server, which has currently been tested with 512 GB of RAM in the 64 bit version of the product.

Question 6 - Administration

Which of the following is not a valid SQL Server 2000 server role?

Choose one of the answers below:

1. Database Administrators
2. Bulk Insert Administrators
3. System Administrators
4. Setup Administrators

Answer:

1. Database Administrators

SQL Server server roles allow you to set global rights for an individual SQL Server. Valid server roles are shown in the below table.

Server role	Description
sysadmin	Can perform any activity in SQL Server.
serveradmin	Can set serverwide configuration options, shut down the server.
setupadmin	Can manage linked servers and startup procedures.
securityadmin	Can manage logins and CREATE DATABASE permissions, also read error logs and change passwords.
processadmin	Can manage processes running in SQL Server.
dbcreator	Can create, alter, and drop databases.
diskadmin	Can manage disk files.
Bulkadmin	Can execute BULK INSERT statements.

Question 7 - Administration

Which of the following is not a valid SQL Server 2000 database role?

Choose one of the answers below:

1. public
2. db_owner
3. db_accessadmin
4. db_datareader
5. db_bulkadmin

Answer:

5. db_bulkadmin

A database role lets you assign rights to an individual database user. In the below table, you can see a list of valid database roles:

Database roles	Description
db_owner	Performs the activities of all database roles.The permissions of this role span all of the other fixed database roles.
db_accessadmin	Adds or removes NT 4.0 or Windows 2000 groups and users, and SQL Server users in the database.
db_datareader	Sees all data from all user tables in the database.
db_datawriter	Adds, changes, or deletes data from all user tables in the database.
db_ddladmin	Adds, modifies, or drops objects in the database (runs all DDLs).
db_securityadmin	Manages roles and members of SQL Server 2000 database roles, and manages statement and object permissions in the database.
db_backupoperator	Has permission to back up the database.
db_denydatareader	Denies permission to select data in the database.
db_denydatawriter	Denies permission to change data in the database.

Question 8 - Administration

You have added John into the sysadmin server role of your SQL Server. John is also a member of the accounting database role which has been denied access to the Salaries table inside the Employees database. What will John's effective permissions be?

Choose one of the answers below:

1. John would have no access to the Employees database.
2. John would be able to read the Salaries table but not update, delete or write to it.
3. John would have full access to the table.
4. John would have access to the Employees database but not the Salaries table.

Answer:

3. John would have full access to the table.

Since John is in the sysadmin server role, all other rights are superceeded and he is granted full control of your SQL Server.

Question 9 - Administration

What is the most likely reason for receiving the following error when signing in with the sa account?
Login failed- User: Reason: Not defined as a valid user of a trusted SQL Server connection.

Choose one of the answers below:

1. The account your application is using doesn't have the appropriate SQL Server permissions.
2. Your domain account does not have log on locally rights.
3. SQL Server is set to Mixed Authentication mode.
4. SQL Server is set to Windows Only Authentication
5. SQL Server's master database is corrupt

Answer:

4. SQL Server is set to Windows Only Authentication

During installation, SQL Server will ask you what authentication type you would like to setup for the server, SQL Server and Windows or Windows Only. The default option is Windows Only. If you specify this option, then you will be unable to connect to the SQL Server with SQL Server authentication. You would receive this error if you connected to SQL Server for sa for example.

Question 10 - Administration

You are a SQL Server administrator that has received a number of calls about slow database performance querying the SALES table. You suspect that the problem is fragmentation of the data. What is the easiest way to prove that the table is fragmented and look at the page density.

Choose one of the answers below:

1. Enterprise Manager
2. PerfMon (System Monitor)
3. Use a DBCC Command
4. Use a system stored procedure
5. None of the above solutions will tell you fragmentation

Answer:

3. Use a DBCC Command

DBCC SHOWCONTIG is the best way to research page fragmentation and density. In SQL Server 7.0 and 2000, there is no way to see the statistics as easily as the SHOWCONTIG command. Perfmon will show pages a second but not density of the data.

See DBCC Showcontig.

Question 11 - Administration

You receive a call from a network administrator complaining about the amount of ping type traffic from your machine to the SQL Servers. You determine that it is most likely being caused by Enterprise Manager polling the SQL Servers to see if they're still online. How would you disable polling inside Enterprise Manager?

Choose one of the answers below:

1. You can't disable this in Enterprise Manager
2. Go to Tools | Options in Enterprise Manager and uncheck "Poll server to find out state and related service" in the general tab.
3. Right-click on Management, then Options and unselect "Poll server to find out state and related service".
4. Right-click on the SQL Server you wish to stop polling on, go to properties and unselect "Poll server to find out state and related service" in the General tab.
5. Go to File | Options and select "Poll server to find out state and related service" in the Tools tab.

Answer:

2. Go to Tools | Options in Enterprise Manager and uncheck "Poll server to find out state and related service" in the general tab.

Enterprise Manager will by default poll the SQL Servers you have registered in Enterprise Manager every 10 seconds. It polls them to see if the service is running our not. Polling doesn't take up a lot of traffic, but it can be an annoyance to some network administrators. To quickly disable it in Enterprise Manager go to Tools | Options in Enterprise Manager and uncheck "Poll server to find out state and related service".

Question 12 - Administration

You are trying to use SQL Server 2000 Enterprise Manager in a rather slow network. Every time you try to connect to a new SQL Server, Enterprise Manager times out in 4 seconds. How can you increase this connection time-out setting so you can manage the servers in this environment?

Choose one of the answers below:

1. Go to File | Options in Enterprise Manager and increase the timeout setting in the Login Time-out (seconds) setting in the Tools tab.
2. Go to Tools | Options in Enterprise Manager and increase the timeout setting in the Login Time-out (seconds) setting in the Advanced tab.
3. Go to Tools | Options in Enterprise Manager and increase the timeout setting in the Query Time-out (seconds) setting in the Advanced tab.
4. Go to File | Options in Enterprise Manager and increase the timeout setting in the Query Time-out (seconds) setting in the Tools tab.
5. Edit the Timeout DWORD in the HKEY_LOCAL_MACHINE\SOFTWARE\Microsoft\Microsoft SQL Server registry key.

Answer:

2. Go to Tools | Options in Enterprise Manager and increase the timeout setting in the Login Time-out (seconds) setting in the Advanced tab.

The default connection time-out setting in SQL Server is 4 seconds. While this is fine in most environments, slow networks or connecting to a SQL Server across the Internet may require more time than 4 seconds. To fix this go to Tools | Options in Enterprise Manager and increase the Login time-out setting in the Advanced tab.

Question 13 - Administration

You have a Windows 2000 Advanced Server running in per processor licensing mode for SQL Server 2000. You machine currently is licensed for and running 4 processors when you upgrade it to 8. Both the OS and SQL Server see the processors fine. How do you change the license count used by SQL Server?
Contributed by David Benoit.

Choose one of the answers below:

1. Re-run setup and select Advanced Options, Change Licensing and add the appropriate amount of processors.
2. Re-run setup and select Change Installation. Then select the appropriate amount of processors for your server to license.
3. Go to Add/Remove Programs in Control Panel. Then select SQL Server and when the wizard comes up, select Change Installation, then select the appropriate amount of processors.
4. Go to Control Panel and select SQL Server 2000 Licensing Setup. Adjust the processor count to the appropriate amount.
5. Go to Control Panel and select Licensing. Adjust the processor count to the appropriate amount.

Answer:

4. Go to Control Panel and select SQL Server 2000 Licensing Setup. Adjust the processor count to the appropriate amount.

Once you install SQL Server 2000, a new applet will appear in your Control Panel where you can adjust the licensing of your SQL Server after your installation. To adjust the licensing, go to SQL Server 2000 Licensing Setup in the Control Panel. The Licensing applet in the control panel handles most other Microsoft licensing.

Question 14 - Administration

How many instances of SQL Server 7.0 can you run on a single Window 2000 Advanced Server that is not clustered.

Choose one of the answers below:

1. 1
2. 2
3. 8
4. 16
5. Unlimitted

Answer:

1. 1

You can only run one instance of SQL Server 7.0 in a normal non-clustered environment. If you'd like to run more than one instance, you must upgrade to SQL Server 2000. SQL Server 2000 can support up to 16 instances of SQL Server, one of which can be a SQL Server 7.0 instance (if it's set to be the default instance).

Question 15 - Administration

What does the 10 represent in the following command in SQL Server 2000?
DBCC SHRINKDATABASE (Northwind, 10)

Choose one of the answers below:

1. The 10 means you wish to have shrink the database to where it will be 10MB.
2. The 10 means you wish to have only 10 percent of empy space after the shrinkage is complete
3. The 10 means you wish to shrink the database by 10 MB.
4. The 10 means you wish to shrink the database by 10 percent of its current size.
5. The 10 means you wish to shrink the database by 10 data pages.

Answer:

2. The 10 means you wish to have only 10 percent of empy space after the shrinkage is complete

The DBCC SHRINKDATABASE command will shrink the database to a target size in percentage. To call it simply pass it the database name and the percentage you wish to leave free.
Reference : DBCC SHRINKDATABASE in Books Online

Question 16 - Administration

You have a Windows 2000 Advanced Edition Server with 16 GB of RAM in it and the proper switches set in the Boot.ini file. The server is running SQL Server 2000 Enterprise Edition with AWE enabled to utilize the extended RAM. How much RAM can the SQL Server see?

Choose one of the answers below:

1. None of the below
2. 2 GB
3. 4 GB
4. 8 GB
5. 16 GB
6. 32 GB

Answer:

4. 8 GB

SQL Server 2000 can only see 8GB of RAM with Windows 2000 Advanced Server. To see the full amount of RAM (up to 64GB), you must run Windows 2000 DataCenter Edtion.

Reference (Books Online) : Maximum Capacity Specifications

Question 17 - Administration

You recently became a SQL Server administrator at Incompetent Inc. One of the servers that you inherited was recently rebuilt with Windows 2000 Server (sometimes referred to Windows 2000 Server Standard Edition). The server is an 8-processor machine and is running SQL Server 2000 Enterprise Edition. How many processors can SQL Server utilize on this machine?

Choose one of the answers below:

1. 1
2. 2
3. 4
4. 8
5. You can't run Enterprise Edition of SQL Server 2000 on Standard Editon of Windows 2000 Server.

Answer:

3. 4

SQL Server 2000 Enterprise Edition can utilize all the processors that Windows 2000 can utilize. In this case however, Windows 2000 Server (Standard Edition) can only utilize 4 processors. We probably need to have another option to send the person who rebuilt the 8-way server using Windows 2000 Server (Standard Edition) back to training.
Reference : See Maximum Capacity Specifications in Books Online.

Question 18 - Administration

You are installing SQL Server 2000 on a Windows 2000 machine. The installation fails midway through the setup and after a reboot, you wish to research the installation problem in Books Online before trying again. Where could you find Books Online?

Choose one of the answers below:

1. The temp directory
2. The install directory on the server
3. Another SQL Server 2000 machine
4. The SQL Server 2000 CD-ROM
5. All the above

Answer:

3. Another SQL Server 2000 machine

Unlike SQL Server 7.0, the Books Online files for SQL Server 2000 can't be found on the install CD. Instead, you would have to turn to a server that already has SQL Server installed to see Books Online. Another option is to download the service pack 3 upgraded Books Online from Microsoft.

Question 19 - Administration

You are about to migrate your SQL Server 6.5 databases to SQL Server 2000 using the SQL Server Upgrade Wizard. Which of the following is not a requirement when running the SQL Server Upgrade Wizard to migrate a SQL Server 6.5 database to SQL Server 2000?

Choose one of the answers below:

1. Stop replication and ensure the log is empty
2. The tempdb database must be at least 5 MB in size
3. The master database must have at least 3 MB of free space
4. You will need space to accomodate approximately 1.5 times the size of the SQL Server 6.5 databases
5. You should disable all startup stored procedures

Answer:

2. The tempdb database must be at least 5 MB in size

The SQL Server Upgrade Wizard requires at least 10 MB in the tempdb database to properly run. It is recommended however that you have at least 25 MB in the tempdb database.
Reference : Upgrade from v6.5
How to Upgrade SQL Server 6.5 and 7.0 to SQL Server 2000.

Question 20 - Administration

When performing a security audit of your SQL Server environment you notice that a user named Mary has been denied access to the Orders table. Mary's login has also been granted bulkadmin server role authority. What could be said about Mary's permissions?

Choose one of the answers below:

1. Mary would never be able to insert any new data into the table
2. Mary would always be able to insert new data into the table
3. Mary would only be able to bulk insert new data into the table
4. Mary would be able to insert but not BULK INSERT into the table
5. None of the above

Answer:

1. Mary would never be able to insert any new data into the table

SQL Server server roles give a user predefined rights at a server and database level. Mary's underlying rights will override her server role rights in this case however. The bulkadmin server role depends on Mary to have rights to the underlying table that she wishes to issue a BULK INSERT into.

Question 21 - Administration

You add an additional 8 GB of RAM to a Windows 2000 Advanced Server, bringing it up to a total of 16 GB of RAM. After rebooting, you notice that SQL Server 2000 Enterprise Edition (32 bit) does not seem to be utilizing the new RAM. What would be the first thing to check to get SQL Server 2000 Enterprise Edition to utilize all 16 GB?

Choose one of the answers below:

1. Set the AWE Enabled
2. Set the /pae switch in the boot.ini file
3. Set the /3GB switch in the boot.ini file
4. Set SQL Server to use fixed RAM, not dynamic
5. The above specification can't use this amount of RAM

Answer:

5. The above specification can't use this amount of RAM

The 32 bit version of SQL Server 2000 Enterprise Edition can only see 8 GB of RAM. Adding the additional RAM to this machine (if it was dedicated to SQL Server) would not be a wise investment. To use the additional RAM, you would need to upgrade to the 64 bit version of SQL Server or go to DataCenter Edition of Windows. Reference: Maximum Capacity Specifications.

Question 22 - Administration

You are a DBA who is taking over a job after a consultant has left. When auditing disaster recovery scripts, you find the below script on the consultants workstation. What would be the result if you execute it?

```
USE master
EXEC sp_addmessage 6000, 16,
   N'An error has occured in %s. Please
resubmit the query',
   'us_english',
   'true',
   'replace'
```

Choose one of the answers below:

1. A custom error 6000 would be created at severity 16 in English. The error would be written out to the Windows event log.
2. A custom error 16 would be created at severity 6000 in English. The error would be written out to the Windows event log.
3. A custom error 6000 would be created at severity 16 in English. The error would not be written out to the Windows event log.
4. A custom error 16 would be created at severity 6000 in English. The error would not be written out to the Windows event log.
5. The script would not execute and return an error.

Answer:

5. The script would not execute and return an error.

The above script would fail to execute since the error number specified in the first parameter fell into the range of errors reserved for the system messages. User-defined error messages must have an ID greater than 50000.

Reference: Books Online "sp_addmessage".

Question 23 - Administration

What will be the complete result of executing the following query in SQL Server 2000?

```
ALTER DATABASE Northwind
SET SINGLE_USER
WITH ROLLBACK AFTER 30 SECONDS
```

Choose one of the answers below:

1. The Northwind database will be placed in single user mode after 30 seconds
2. The Northwind database will be placed in single user mode and everyone will be disconnected after 30 seconds of executing the above query
3. The Northwind database will be placed in single user mode
4. The Northwind database will be placed in single user mode and users will receive a warning to disconnect in 30 seconds
5. An error

Answer:

2. The Northwind database will be placed in single user mode and everyone will be disconnected after 30 seconds of executing the above query

The query will place the database in single user mode and give users 30 seconds to disconnect. If they don't disconnect, their connection is terminated. There is no visual warning during this duration. No new users are allowed in during that specified time either.

Reference : Books Online "Alter Database".

Question 24 - Administration

What is not a way to stop SQL Server 2000?

Choose one of the answers below:

1. By using SQL Server Enterprise Manager.
2. By using net stop mssqlserver from a command prompt.
3. By using Services in Control Panel.
4. By using SQL Server Service Manager
5. The SHUTDOWN T-SQL Command.
6. All the above are ways to stop SQL Server.

Answer:

6. All the above are ways to stop SQL Server.

All the above ways are methods to stop a SQL Server.

Question 25 - Administration

You are a SQL Server developer who is programming a query to read a file from a different server in the same domain name using a UNC path and perform an action on that file. You run the xp_cmdshell stored procedure from a server called Alpha to obtain a directory listing on the server called Beta and a share called temp. Both Alpha and Beta are Windows 2003 servers and you're logged in with a sysadmin account. When running the query you get the follwing results:

```
xp_cmdshell 'dir \\Beta\temp'
```

Logon failure: unknown user name or bad password.
(2 row(s) affected)

What is the most likely cause of this problem?

Choose one of the answers below:

1. The xp_cmdshell stored procedure can't see UNC paths
2. The temp share is invalid
3. The login that you're signing into SQL Server with doesn't have permissions to xp_cmdshell
4. The account that starts SQL Server doesn't have permissions to the temp share
5. The proxy account in SQL Server Agent has an invalid password

Answer:

4. The account that starts SQL Server doesn't have permissions to the temp share

The problem is likely a permission problem with the account that starts SQL Server. Typically, you may see this if the account that starts SQL Server is the localsystem account, which can't leave the local server. XP_cmdshell can indeed see UNC paths and if the UNC path was invalid, you would receive an error stating the network path couldn't be found.

Question 26 - Administration

You are a purchasing manager trying to determine how many SQL Server 2000 licenses you will need to purchase in your environment.You have a two-node Windows 2000 cluster running 3 instances of SQL Server 2000 (clustered). One instance is on a server called Node1, the other two are on a server called Node2. Each server has 4 processors and you want to comply with the per-processor licensing model for SQL Server 2000. What is the minimum amount of processor licenses would you need to buy for this production environment?

Choose one of the answers below:

1. You would have to license 8 processors for Enterprise Edition of SQL Server
2. You would have to license 4 processors for Enterprise Edition of SQL Server
3. You would have to license 12 processors for Enterprise Edition of SQL Server
4. You would have to license 8 processors for Standard Edition of SQL Server
5. You would have to license 4 processors for Standard Edition of SQL Server
6. You would have to license 12 processors for Standard Edition of SQL Server

Answer:

1. You would have to license 8 processors for Enterprise Edition of SQL Server

You would need to license 2 intances of SQL Server in this multiple-instance cluster or 8 processors. Since your SQL Server is clustered, your server must run SQL Server 2000 Enterprise Edition. The third instance does not need to be licensed since you are running Enterprise Edition of SQL Server.

Reference : SQL ServerLicensing FAQ

Question 27 - Administration

You are a SQL Server administrator who has recently set up a personal SQL Server for a developer with 256 databases installed on it. The developer's operating system is Windows 2000 Workstation running SQL Server 2000 Desktop Edition with the default server and databases options. When the developer expands the list of databases in Enterprise Manager after starting his SQL Server for the first time, it takes a long time to retrieve the list of databases (4 minutes). What is most likely the cause of the slowdown?

Choose one of the answers below:

1. SQL Server Desktop Edition only supports 200 databases on a single server
2. The Auto Close database option is enabled on the databases
3. The Auto Shrink database option is enabled on the databases
4. The Auto Grow File data file option is enabled on the databases
5. The Torn Page Detection database option is enabled

Answer:

2. The Auto Close database option is enabled on the databases

The most likely cause of the slowdown is that the Auto Close option is enabled. When you first access the database list, the databases have to be opened and this takes time. The default option of Desktop Edition is to have this option enabled. While having Auto Shrink enabled may slow down a system if a shrink is in progress, it wouldn't cause a slowdown in pulling a database list.

Question 28 - Administration

You are a SQL Server administrator who wants to expand the amount of memory your SQL Server has available to it. Your Windows machine currently has 512 MB of RAM and you wish to expand by a sizable amount. At what memory point would you set the /PAE switch in the boot.ini to access extended RAM in the 32-bit Windows architecture?

Choose one of the answers below:

1. More than 2 GB
2. More than 4 GB
3. More than 8 GB
4. More than 16 GB
5. More than 32 GB
6. More than 64 GB

Answer:

2. More than 4 GB

The /PAE (Physical Addressing Extension) switch in the boot.ini allows Windows to extend past the boundary of the 32-bit memory limit of four gigabytes (GB). By setting the switch, Windows 2000 Advanced Server can extend to 8 GB of RAM and DataCenter Edition can extend to 64 GB of RAM. The boot.ini file can be found in the root of your system drive.

For more information seehttp://support.microsoft.com/default.aspx?scid=kb;en-us;268363.

Question 29 - Administration

You are in the process of performing an audit for a SQL Server 7.0 to 2000 conversion. You want to ensure that the same options are enabled in SQL Server 2000 that were enabled in SQL Server 7.0. What SQL Server 2000 recovery model does the following SQL Server 7.0 database options translate into?

Truncate on Checkpoint : On
Select Into/Bulkcopy : Off
Auto Close : Off
Auto Update Statistics : On

Choose one of the answers below:

1. Full Recovery Model
2. Bulk-logged Recovery Model
3. Simple Recovery Model
4. Automatic Recovery Model

Answer:

3. Simple Recovery Model

Only two of the options that are enabled apply to the recovery model. If truncate on checkpoint is enabled, then this translates to Simple Recovery Model. If it is disabled, it translates into Full Recovery Model or Bulk-Logged, dependent on whether Select Into/Bulkcopy was also enabled. Reference : SQL Server 2000 and SQL Server version 7.0 in Book Online.

Question 30 - Administration

You create a new linked server to Analysis Server 2000 in Enterprise Manager from a SQL Server 2000 server. You set the following options and query:

Linked server: olap
Provider Name: Microsoft OLEDB provider for Olap Services 8.0
Data Source: your OLAP server name
Catalog: FoodMart 2000

```
select *
from openquery(olap, '
select {{[Measures].members} * {[Product].
[Product Family].members}} on columns,
{{([Customers].[All Customers].[USA],
[Education Level].[All Education Level].
[Bachelors Degree] ), ([Customers].[All
Customers].[USA], [Education Level].[All
Education Level].[High School Degree] )},
([Customers].[All Customers].[Canada],
[Education Level].[All Education Level].
[Bachelors Degree] )} on rows from Sales')
```

What is most likely the problem when you get this error?

Could not create an instance of OLE DB provider 'MSOLAP'.
OLE DB error trace [Non-interface error: CoCreate of DSO for MSOLAP returned 0x80040154].

Choose one of the answers below:

1. The MDX is wrong
2. You should have set Product Name: MSOLAP
3. You need service pack 3 of Analysis Services
4. You need to set "AllowInProcess" in Provider Options
5. The SQL server Service account does not have rights to Foodmart 2000

Answer:

4. You need to set "AllowInProcess" in Provider Options

You need to set "AllowInProcess" in Provider options when you create the linked server This may be set already but isn't by default. Note that this will effect all linked servers! Read more here : http://msdn.microsoft.com/library/default.asp?url=/library/en-us/olapdmad/aghtconfig_15bm.asp The MDX is right, you don't need to specify product name, this works on older service packs and you get a different error if the account does not have rights

Question 31 - Administration

You have SQL Server 7.0 merge replication installed in your SQL Server environment. You plan a migration to SQL Server 2000 to receive the better merge replication features. Which server must be upgraded first?

Choose one of the answers below:

1. Upgrade the Publisher server first.
2. Upgrade the Subscriber server first.
3. Upgrade the Distributor server first.
4. Upgrade replication servers in any order.
5. Replication will have to be recreated after the upgrade.

Answer:

3. Upgrade the Distributor server first.

When upgrading servers running replication, whether a service pack upgrade or a full version release, you must upgrade the Distributor first. For replication topologies based on transactional replication with read-only Subscribers, you can upgrade the Subscriber before or after the Publisher and Distributor. For replication topologies based on merge replication or transactional replication with updating Subscribers, you must upgrade the Subscriber after the Publisher and Distributor. Note In many cases, especially in merge replication, the Distributor and Publisher are on the same server and are upgraded at the same time.

Question 32 - Administration

You are an unfortunate DBA who works for Incompetent Inc. You receive a page on Friday that one of your production server's SQL Server 2000 service won't start and is receiving the error "SQL Server evaluation period has expired." What is the most likely cause and how would you fix it with the least amount of effort and data loss?

Choose one of the answers below:

1. Someone installed the Evaluation Edition of SQL Server. To fix, run the installation from the Retail CD.
2. Someone installed the Evaluation Edition of SQL Server. To fix, uninstall SQL Server and then reinstall.
3. You have run out of connection licenses in SQL Server. Go to Licenses in the Control Panel in increase the licenses.
4. Someone installed a MSDN version of SQL Server. To fix, run the installation from the Retail CD.
5. Someone installed the MSDN version of SQL Server. To fix, uninstall SQL Server and then reinstall.

Answer:

1. Someone installed the Evaluation Edition of SQL Server. To fix, run the installation from the Retail CD.

From Microsoft article Q281574: After the SQL Server 2000 Evaluation Edition expires, you can use retail installation to upgrade the expired SQL Server instance to SQL Server 2000 Retail version. To do this, follow these steps:

Run the installation from the Retail Setup CD (for example, a valid Retail Version from the SQL Server 2000 Setup CD).
Select **Upgrade, remove, or add components to an existing instance of SQL Server.**
Choose the instance to upgrade.
Select the **Upgrade your existing installation** option.
Select the **Yes, upgrade my programs** box.
If you do not want to add any additional component, select **No** in the **Do you want to install additional components?** dialog box. If you would like to add more components, select **Yes** and check the boxes for the components you would like to add.
Click **Finish**.
Stop and restart SQL Server.

http://support.microsoft.com/default.aspx?scid=kb;en-us;281574

Question 33 - Administration

You have a SQL Server stored procedure named myStoredProc_sp that runs several audits of the server that you would like to execute every time your SQL Server 2000 machine starts up. How could you accomplish this task via T-SQL?

Choose one of the answers below:

1. exec sp_procoption 'myStoredProc_sp', 'startup', true from the user database.
2. The stored procedure must be in the master database and then run exec sp_procoption 'myStoredProc_sp', 'startup', true
3. Add the keyword of SET STARTUP ON at the first line of the stored procedure
4. Add the keyword of SET STARTUP_OPTION ON at the first line of the stored procedure
5. This is not allowed in SQL Server 2000

Answer:

2. The stored procedure must be in the master database and then run exec sp_procoption 'myStoredProc_sp', 'startup', true

Using the stored procedure: sp_procoption in SQL Server 2000 will allow you to set the stored procedure to execute at SQL Server's startup. The T-SQL procedure must be installed in the master database. You can set this option via Enterprise Manager when editing the stored procedure as an additional check-box also.

Question 34 - Administration

You think you may have a configuration problem where your application may be setting options using the SET command and a user is receiving incorrect answers to his queries because of this. Which of the following commands could tell you what user options are active at a user-connection level for the current connection?

Choose one of the answers below:

1. DBCC USEROPTIONS
2. SET USEROPTIONS
3. SET OPTIONS
4. SP_CONFIGURE
5. SP_DBOPTION

Answer:

1. DBCC USEROPTIONS

The DBCC USEROPTIONS returns the SET options active (set) for the current connection. DBCC USEROPTIONS permissions default to any user. The SP_DBOPTION stored procedure would return database options set at a database-level and the SP_CONFIGURE stored procedure would return options set at a server-level.

Reference: DBCC Useroptions - http://msdn.microsoft.com/library/default.asp?url=/library/en-us/tsqlref/ts_dbcc_4vhv.asp.

Question 35 - Administration

You'd like to load lots of historical data into a table called CustomerHistory using the INSERT T-SQL statement. You wish to temporarily disable all foreign key constraints on the table since this is an archive database and you orphaned records are acceptable for this one load only. Which T-SQL statement would temporarily allow you to accomplish this task?

Choose one of the answers below:

1. ALTER TABLE CustomerHistory NOCHECK CONSTRAINT all
2. ALTER TABLE CustomerHistory CHECK CONSTRAINT all
3. DROP CONSTRAINT ALL on CustomerHistory
4. Use an index hint
5. You can't temporarily disable foreign key constraints

Answer:

1. ALTER TABLE CustomerHistory NOCHECK CONSTRAINT all

It's never recommended to disable foreign key constraints since they've been created for a reason. If you must disable foreign keys you can disable all the foreign keys in a given table by using the ALTER TABLE syntax and using the NOCHECK keyword.

Reference: Alter Table - http://msdn.microsoft.com/library/default.asp?url=/library/en-us/tsqlref/ts_aa-az_3ied.asp.

Question 36 - Administration

What database option could have the most substantial negative effect on database performance in production and shouldn't be enabled in that type of environment?

Choose one of the answers below:

1. READ_ONLY
2. TORN_PAGE_DETECTION
3. AUTO_SHRINK
4. RECOVERY FULL
5. AUTO_UPDATE_STATISTICS

Answer:

3. AUTO_SHRINK

The AUTO_SHRINK option could have the most negative impact on a production database. This is because a database shrink could be issued during the middle of production queries, causing slowdowns or locking issues. Typically you would schedule database shrinks for off hours. The AUTO_CLOSE option is also a negative impact to production as whenever all users are disconnected, the database will close. Reopening it causes a delay in response from the server.

Read only doesn't impact the performance of the server, just prevents writes. This is an option you may want enabled in production.

Recovery full isn't an option and Auto_Update_Statistics is recommended as being left on to ensure the query optimizer has reliable statistics for queries. Torn page detection should always be enabled to prevent corruption, and this doesn't negatively impact production servers.

Question 37 - Administration

You want to create a database backup on a file share on another server. You execute a command similar to this:

```
backup database databasename to
disk='\\nodename\sharename\databasename.bak'
```

but you get an error similar to:

```
Server: Msg 3201, Level 16, State 1, Line 1
Cannot open backup device
'\\nodename\sharename\databasename.bak'. Device error
or device off-line.
See the SQL Server error log for more details.
Server: Msg 3013, Level 16, State 1, Line 1 BACKUP
DATABASE is terminating abnormally.
```

What is likely to be the problem? You may assume the node and share really exist and that there's space available. (Contributed by Darwin Hatheway)

Choose one of the answers below:

1. You must map the share to a drive-letter before you can access it because \\\sharename semantics are not supported by SQL Server
2. The Account that runs the SQL Server service does not have access to that share.
3. SQL Server will only write backups to locally attached disks.
4. You must first configure a backup device to that share and filename by mapping the drive and using sp_addumpdevice.
5. It's probably just a random network error, try the operation again.

Answer:

2. The Account that runs the SQL Server service does not have access to that share.

The Account that runs the SQL Server service does not have access to that share. Is your SQL Server running from a LocalSystemAccount? If so, it will not get access to resources on other nodes. If you want to access resources on other nodes, you must configure your SQL Server to run from a Domain Account with appropriate access to other servers. If you are running with a Domain Account, check to make sure this account has authorization to write to that share.

Question 38 - Administration

You've purchased some new disk drives and installed them in your server to increase disk capacity. They set up as devices H: and I:. You intend to create all new databases on these disks (databases on H and logs on I). How do you adjust SQL Server 2000 to create all new databases on those disks by default?

Choose one of the answers below:

1. Start SQL Enterprise Manager. Right-click on the server of interest and select "Properties" from the context menu. Select "Database Settings" from the dialog box that pops up and adjust the "Default data directory" and "Default log directory" settings to meet your needs.
2. You can't change the default data directory
3. Rerun setup and select Advanced Options. Change the data directory for data and logs and select OK.
4. Change the CustomDataDir data item in registry key: HKEY_LOCAL_MACHINE\SOFTWARE\Microsoft\Microsoft SQL Server\80\Tools\SQLEW
5. Change the SourceDir data item in registry key: HKEY_LOCAL_MACHINE\SOFTWARE\Microsoft\MSSQLServer\Setup

Answer:

1. Start SQL Enterprise Manager. Right-click on the server of interest and select "Properties" from the context menu. Select "Database Settings" from the dialog box that pops up and adjust the "Default data directory" and "Default log directory" settings to meet your needs.

To do this, start SQL Enterprise Manager. Right-click on the server of interest and select "Properties" from the context menu. Select "Database Settings" from the dialog box that pops up and adjust the "Default data directory" and "Default log directory" settings to meet your needs.

Question 39 - Administration

What does the HOST_NAME() function do?

Choose one of the answers below:

1. Equivalent of running SP_WHO
2. Returns the Windows name of the SQL Server computer.
3. Returns your SQL Server's computer name
4. Returns the computer name of the computer that submitted the query
5. This system function doesn't exist

Answer:

4. Returns the computer name of the computer that submitted the query

The HOST_NAME() system function returns the computer name of the computer that runs the query. It's useful if you want to audit who inserted data into a table or for auditing purposes.

Question 40 - Administration

What does the SQLDiag support utility <u>*not*</u> *produce in SQL Server 2000?*

Choose one of the answers below:

1. Registry information
2. Text of all SQL Server error logs
3. IRQ and port report
4. The last 500 queries and exceptions
5. All the above are produced

Answer:

4. The last 500 queries and exceptions

When you would like to send information to a SQL Server support person, the best report to run is SQLDiag.exe. It produces a number of things but it does only produce the last 100 queries, not 500.

SQL Server Operations Guide - http://www.microsoft.com/technet/prodtechnol/sql/2000/maintain/sqlops5.mspx

Question 41 - Data Warehousing\Business Intelligence

You are a DTS developer who would like to deploy a DTS package with 10 database connections to 50 servers on a regular basis. You would like to be able to dynamically change where the DTS package connects to without having to go to each connection. The method you plan to do that with is to update a Global Variable with the server name which would then in turn update the connections at runtime. How do you dynamically change in SQL Server 7.0 the connection to the Global Variable's parameter?

Choose one of the answers below:

1. ActiveX Script Task
2. Dynamic Properties Task
3. Execute Package Task
4. Data Pump Task
5. Change the Connection to use a UDL file

Answer:

1. ActiveX Script Task

In SQL Server 7.0, the only method to accomplish this task is with the ActiveX Script Task. You can use the DTS object model from within an ActiveX Script Task to change the properties of a task or step. In SQL Server 2000, you have a variety of thepossible options. The easiest method in SQL Server 2000 is with the Dynamic Properties Task. This did not exist in SQL Server 7.0 however.

Question 42 - Data Warehousing\Business Intelligence

How do you determine what service pack you're on in Analysis Services 2000?

Choose one of the answers below:

1. Open Analysis Manager, right-click on Analysis Servers under Console Root and select About Analysis Services.
2. Open Analysis Manager and select Help About Analysis Servers.
3. Go to the MDX query tool and run SELECT @@VERSION.
4. Connect to the Analysis Server in Query Analzyer and run SELECT @@VERSION.
5. All the above

Answer:

1. Open Analysis Manager, right-click on Analysis Servers under Console Root and select About Analysis Services.

In the SQL Server 2000 release of Analysis Services, you must Open analysis Manager, right-click on Analysis Servers under Console Root and select About Analysis Services to determine the version of Analysis Services you're currently running.
Reference : Service pack installation readme file.

Question 43 - Disaster Recovery

Your production SQL Server running SQL Server SP2 has a motherboard failure that requires you to transfer your inventory database called Inventory over to a new server. Your application logs into the database with the login name of webuser. To restore the application to it's previous state, you create the webuser login in the new environment. You take the most recent SQL Server complete database backup of the Inventory database from tape and restore it onto an another existing server. After the restore, you test the applicaiton only to receive the following error:

```
Server: Msg 916, Level 14, State 1, Line 1
Server user 'webuser' is not a valid user in
database 'Inventory'.
```

You confirm in Enterprise Manager that the webuser login has been created and that the webuser user is in the Inventory database. The user though appears not to have a login associated with it though. What is the best way to fix the problem and restore access to the application?

Choose one of the answers below:

1. Delete the user and recreate it.
2. Run *sp_change_users_login 'auto_fix', webuser* while in the Inventory database.
3. Restore the master database
4. Run *sp_adduser webuser* while in the Inventory database.
5. Run *sp_associatelogin webuser, webuser* while in the Inventory database.

Answer:

2. Run *sp_change_users_login 'auto_fix', webuser* while in the Inventory database.

After you restore a database from a different server, the login SID will not match the old login SID from the old machine. For more information on this problem and solution see this article.

Question 44 - DTS

Which of the following is not a phase in DTS' multiphase data pump.

Choose one of the answers below:

1. On Pump Complete
2. On Batch Complete
3. Post Source Data
4. Pre Source Phase
5. Data Copy Phase

Answer:

5. Data Copy Phase

Valid phases in the multiphase data pump are : Pre Source, Row Transform, Post Row Transform, On Batch Complete, Post Source Data, On Pump Complete. There are also some subphases.

See Chapter 21 - Monitoring the DTS Multiphase Data Pump in Visual Basic - http://www.microsoft.com/resources/documentation/sql/2000/all/reskit/en-us/part5/c2161.mspx

Question 45 - DTS

You are a DTS developer who has just installed SQL Server Personal Edition and are trying to convert data from Access to SQL Server using the Transform Data task while cleansing the data using the multi-phase feature. For some reason though, you cannot see any of the individual phases when in the Transform Data task under the Transformations tab. How would you make it where you can see the feature?

Choose one of the answers below:

1. Upgrade to Standard Edition
2. Ugrade to Enterprise or Developer Edition
3. Enable it by going to Package | Package Properties inside the DTS package and selecting the appropriate option under the Advanced tab.
4. Enable the feature in Enterprise Manager by right-clicking on Data Transformation Services | Properties and selecting the appropriate option.
5. You can only use the multi-phase data pump when transforming SQL Server data.

Answer:

4. Enable the feature in Enterprise Manager by right-clicking on Data Transformation Services | Properties and selecting the appropriate option.

To turn on the ability to see the multi-phase data pump feature in DTS Designer, you have to right-click on Data Transformation Services in SQL Server Enterprise Manager and select Properties. Once in the Properties screen select Show Multi-phase Pump in DTS Designer. If this option is disabled, you can still run packages that use the multi-phase data pump feature, you just won't be able to edit it.

Question 46 - DTS

You are a DTS developer who is trying to debug a problem with a step in a DTS package. The server runs SQL Server 2000 Enterprise Edition and the package is executing through a SQL Server Agent job. How would you turn on logging for the DTS package so you can see the success or failure of each step.

Choose one of the answers below:

1. Right-click on the package and select Package Logs. Check Enable Logging and Apply.
2. Right-click on the package and select Package Logs. Select the server name you wish to output the logs to with the user name and password.
3. Reschedule the package with logging. Right-click on the package and select Schedule. Specify the time to schedule the package for and check Enable Logging.
4. Open the package in Enterprise Manager and go to Package | Logging. Select Log package execution to SQL Server and specify a server, user name and password to log to. Save the package.
5. Open the package in Enterprise Manager and go to Package | Properties. Under the Logging tab, select Log package execution to SQL Server and specify a server, user name and password to log to. Save the package.

Answer:

5. Open the package in Enterprise Manager and go to Package | Properties. Under the Logging tab, select Log package execution to SQL Server and specify a server, user name and password to log to. Save the package.

To turn on DTS package logging, open the package and go to Package | Properties. Under the Logging tab, specify a server, user name and password to log to. To view the logs, right click on the package in Enterprise Manager and select Package Logs. Reference: DTS Best Practices.

Question 47 - DTS

You are a DTS developer who wants to load data from a flat file extract into a SQL Server table. While you're analyzing the data, you know the data is not consistent and you would like all the data in the Name column to be upper-case. During the load, you want to scrub data being inserted into SQL Server. What method would be the fastest way to do this in DTS in one step?

Choose one of the answers below:

1. Bulk Insert Task
2. Transform Data Task (Data Pump Task)
3. ActiveX Script Task
4. Execute SQL Task
5. Execute Process Task

Answer:

2. Transform Data Task (Data Pump Task)

The Transform Data Task (also known as the Data Pump Task) is the only way to perform a data scrubbing function in a single step. This is done through adjusting the Transformation tab in the task to reflect that this column will use the UPPER function instead of a straight copy. You could also have used the Bulk Insert Task to bulk load the data into a staging table then clean it and transfer it but it would not have been in a single step.

Reference:
Transform Data Task.
Mapping Column Transformations.

Question 48 - DTS

You are a DTS developer who is using data link files (UDL) to connect to the source and destination SQL Servers with the default options set. You complete the DTS package and then ship it to a client location for production deployment. The client then changes the UDL file to reflect their server names but the DTS package seems to time out when connecting to the source server. What is the most likely problem?

Choose one of the answers below:

1. The DTS package is caching the UDL file from design time.
2. The proper MDAC drivers are not installed.
3. The user needs an owner password to the package to execute it.
4. The user executing the package must not have the proper permissions.
5. None of the above

Answer:

1. The DTS package is caching the UDL file from design time.

DTS caches UDL files at design time unless you specify to always read from the file at runtime. Since the default options were selected, which does not include the checkbox to read the file at runtime, this is the most likely cause of the package timeout. In other words, the package is still trying to connect to your development server, not the client's production server. While MDAC drivers may possibly be a problem in a named instance, UDL options would be the first place to check.

Reference:
Technet Chat: DTS.
Discussion on this topic..

Question 49 - DTS

Consider the follwing commented MDX statement Executed against the Foodmart 2000 database. You get the following helpful error: "Unable to Open Cellset Formula Error - Unknown Error" What is the most likely cause of the failure? Contributed by Keith Henry

```
select [Measures].[MeasuresLevel].members on columns,
non empty { -- row axis set{ --set 1
 ([Department].[All Department].[HQ Finance and
Accounting],[Store].[All Stores].[USA].[CA]), --tupel
1 ([Department].[All Department].[HQ General
Management],[Store].[All Stores].[USA].[OR]), --tupel
2
([Department].[All Department].[HQ Human Resources],
[Store].[All Stores].[USA].[CA]), --tupel 3
([Department].[All Department].[HQ Information
Systems], [Store].[All Stores].[USA] ),  --tupel 4
([Department].[All Department].[HQ Marketing],
[Store].[All Stores].[USA].[CA])  --tupel 5
} --end set 1, { --set 2           [Department].[All
Department].children * [Store Type].[All Store Type].
children } --end set 2 } on rows
from [HR]
```

Choose one of the answers below:

1. You needed to wrap the "[Measures].[MeasuresLevel]. members" statement with {} because it is an axis
2. The "*" (crossjoin) operator takes two sets, so it should be "{set a} * {set b}" and not "member1 * member2"
3. All the tuples in a set must contain the same dimensions in order to the same level. tupel 4 is a level out.
4. All the sets nested in a set must share the same dimensionality. {set 1} and {set 2} have different dimensionality
5. None of these values return anything and so are removed by the "non empty" keyword

Answer:

4. All the sets nested in a set must share the same dimensionality. {set 1} and {set 2} have different dimensionality

Number 1 is wrong because the .members function returns a set and doesn't need {} delimiters
Number 2 is wrong because the .children function also returns a set (not a member) and doesn't need {} delimiters
Number 3 is wrong because while all the tuples in a set must contains the same dimensions, but it doesn't matter which levels they are at.
Number 5 is wrong because empty cellsets do not return this error and this cellset should be full anyway
Number 4 is correct because {set 1} is a list of tupels all with [Department] & [Store] while {set 2} is a CrossJoin between [Department] & [Store Type] CrossJoin({set A}, {set B}) or {{set A} * {set B}} produces a set containing all the combinations of all the sets A and B in order. Both sets must be mutually exclusive to avoid duplicates. The result set can still be nested within sets and listed next to other sets with the same dimensionality.

Question 50 - DTS

What is the best DTS task to use to execute a batch file and pass in parameters?

Choose one of the answers below:

1. ActiveX Script Task
2. Execute Command Task
3. Data Pump Task
4. Execute SQL Task
5. Execute Process Task

Answer:

5. Execute Process Task

The Execute Process Task has the ability to execute a program of almost any type from a DTS package. You could execute a batch file also through other mechanisms involving ActiveX through the ActiveX Script task, but it would take much more time to develop a solution.

Question 51 - Enterprise Administration

SQL Server in a MSCS cluster can't backup to the local C drive in Enterprise Manager. What is the most likely reason?

Choose one of the answers below:

1. You must first set the SQL Server service to be a dependency of the drives.
2. SQL Server can't see local drives in a cluster
3. The SQL Server service doesn't have permissions to the drive
4. You must first activate the drive in Cluster Administrator
5. Clustered SQL Servers can only see dynamic drives

Answer:

2. SQL Server can't see local drives in a cluster

SQL Server in a cluster can only see drives that are in the cluster group. Local drives cannot be backed up to or used to store data since the other participating nodes can't see it. You must also set the SQL Server service to be a dependency on the drives before the drives can be seen.

See:SQL Server 2000 Failover Clustering

Question 52 - Enterprise Administration

You recently increased the amount of RAM that your SQL Server running Windows 2000 Advanced Server was using to 6GB. You turned on the AWE Enabled using sp_configure and adjusted the maximum amount of memory that SQL Server could use. After stopping and starting the SQL Server instance, it appears that SQL Server is still not using all the memory you specified. What is the most likely cause?

Choose one of the answers below:

1. You must restart the computer.
2. The account that starts SQL Server must have Logon as a Service rights.
3. You must set the memory to use Fixed Memory rather than dynamic memory settings using sp_configure or Server Properties in Enterprise Manager.
4. The account that starts SQL Server must have Lock Page in Memory rights.
5. You can only use AWE memory with DataCenter Edition of SQL Server 2000.

Answer:

4. The account that starts SQL Server must have Lock Page in Memory rights.

For SQL Server Enterprise and Developer Editions to use an extended amount of memory, you must enable SQL Server AWE (Address Windows Extensions). Once you enable it SQL Server will take all but 128 MB of RAM unless you specify a maximum. You must set the Lock Page in Memory option for the account that starts SQL Server for the setting to work. That setting can be found in Local Security Policy Setting console under Administrative Tools.

See How to configure memory for more than 2 GB in SQL Server.

Question 53 - Enterprise Administration

What is the maximum amount of RAM that SQL Server 2000 Enterprise (64-bit) Edition can access in Windows Server 2003 Datacenter Edition?

Choose one of the answers below:

1. 8 GB
2. 16 GB
3. 32 GB
4. 64 GB
5. 512 GB

Answer:

5. 512 GB

Enterprise Edition (64-bit) provide the most scalable data platform to take advantage of the class of Intel Itanium-based servers. Addressing more memory than any other edition of SQL Server, it scales to Up to 64 processors, up to 512 Gb of memory and a maximum database size 1,048,516 TB.

See SQL Server 2000 (64-bit) Product Overview.

Question 54 - Enterprise Administration

How do you properly make MSDTC cluster-aware (make it a clustered resource)?

Choose one of the answers below:

1. Right-click on the Cluster Group in Cluster Administrator and select New Resource. Then select MSDTC as the resource.
2. Right-click on the Cluster Group in Cluster Administrator and select New Resource and then select Generic Service as the resource type.
3. No action required, MSDTC is clustered automatically during the SQL Server install.
4. Run comclust.exe from a command prompt on the primary node.
5. Run comclust.exe from a command prompt on both nodes.

Answer:

5. Run comclust.exe from a command prompt on both nodes.

MSDTC is clustered before installing SQL Server by running comclust.exe from a command prompt on each node. This will create the MSDTC resource in the Cluster Group. For more information on clustering, read the Step by Step Guide to Clustering.

See also Building the SQL Server 2000 Clusters.

Question 55 - Enterprise Administration

In Windows 2000 Advanced Server, where would you go to start the Windows cluster installation with the Cluster Service Configuration Wizard?

Choose one of the answers below:

1. Go to the command prompt and type "CLUSSVR.EXE".
2. Go to Cluster Setup under Administrative Tools and click Install Clustering.
3. Go to Add/Remove Programs and select Cluster Service under Windows Components.
4. Go to Add/Remove Programs and select MSCS Clustering under Windows Components
5. Start up the Windows 2000 CD and select Additional Options | Clustering.

Answer:

3. Go to Add/Remove Programs and select Cluster Service under Windows Components.

To start the Cluster Service Configuration Wizard, simply go to Add/Remove Programs and selecting Cluster Service under Windows Components. For more informaiton on how to cluster SQL Server, please read the Step-by-step instructions on how to cluster article.

Question 56 - Enterprise Administration

You recently have taken over support of a SQL Server 2000 Enterprise Edition machine running Windows 2000 Advanced Server. The server has 8 GB of RAM installed but for some reason SQL Server is only utilizing less than 4 GB. What would the likely cause be?

Choose one of the answers below:

1. SQL Server Enterprise Edition only support 4 GB of RAM
2. You must first upgrade to DataCenter edition of SQL Server to see the extended RAM
3. When going above 4 GB, you have to reinstall SQL Server
4. You must turn on the "Allow Extended Memory" option by using sp_configure
5. You must turn on the "AWE Enabled" option by using sp_configure.

Answer:

5. You must turn on the "AWE Enabled" option by using sp_configure.

SQL Server Enterprise Edition can access extended RAM (more than 4GB) by utilizing the AWE setting. You can set this setting by using sp_configure and it does require a restart of SQL Server. AWE will allow SQL Server to use a lot more memory but make sure you set caps on the maximum and minimum amounts of memory SQL Server is allowed to use. Otherwise, it may be suffocate your other processes on the server. See How to configure memory for more than 2 GB in SQL Server.

Question 57 - Enterprise Administration

Which query will tell you which servers are possible owners of a failover cluster?

Choose one of the answers below:

1. master..xp_getnetname
2. SELECT @@VIRTUALSESRVERS
3. SELECT * FROM ::FN_VIRTUALSERVERNODES()
4. SELECT * FROM ::FN_VIRTUALSERVERS()
5. SELECT * FROM master..SYSSERVERS where srvstatus=1090

Answer:

3. SELECT * FROM ::FN_VIRTUALSERVERNODES()

In a cluster you can run SELECT * FROM :: FN_VIRTUALSERVERNODES() to determine which nodes are possible owners of a failed resource group. It's also useful for debugging possible cluster problems. Reference: FN_VirtualServerNodes.

Question 58 - Enterprise Administration

What is the best way to change what account starts SQL Server 2000 in Windows 2003 Enterprise Edition?

Choose one of the answers below:

1. In the Services applet in Control Panel | Administrative Tools
2. In Enterprise Manager under SQL Server Properties for the server and the Security tab.
3. In Cluster Administrator
4. The Server Manager tool
5. The Server Network Utility tool

Answer:

2. In Enterprise Manager under SQL Server Properties for the server and the Security tab.

The proper way to change what account starts SQL Server on any platform of Windows is through Enterprise Manager. Enterprise Manager will ensure that the proper permissions are given to the account, the login is created and the registry changes are made. Some of these items are missed by the other options listed above.

Reference: How to change the service account.

Question 59 - Enterprise Administration

You have a SQL Server single-instance cluster (active/passive) and are trying to determine how many licenses you're going to need of SQL Server 2000. One server in the cluster has 2 processors and the other has 4 processors. The 2 processor machine is the primary active machine while the 4 processor machine is only a passive node. How many per-processor licenses will you need to purchase?

Choose one of the answers below:

1. 2 processors
2. 4 processors
3. 6 processors
4. 8 processors

Answer:

2. 4 processors

In a single-instance cluster in SQL Server 2000 (previously known as active/passive), you must only license the primary server. The exception to this though is when the secondary server has more processors than the primary. In this case, you must license the differences in processors.

Reference: Licensing SQL Server.

Question 60 - Enterprise Administration

Your SQL Server 2000 (SQL Server service pack 2) fails over to another node in the middle of the night. In researching the failure, you find a "Write Delay Error" in the System event log. What of the following is the first thing you should research when troubleshooting an error like this?

Choose one of the answers below:

1. Microsoft Clustering Services (MSCS)
2. SQL Server
3. Operating System
4. Hardware

Answer:

4. Hardware

When researching clustering problems or mysterious failovers, you should start with what component was installed first. This would mean, you would first troubleshoot the hardware, then the operating system, MSCS and finally SQL Server.

Reference: Troublesooting Clusters - http://support.microsoft.com/default.aspx?kbid=327518.

Question 61 - Enterprise Administration

You have 2 nodes in your Windows 2003 Enterprise Edition cluster. You'd like to determine how many total instances of SQL Server you could install across the cluster if you placed an equal amount of instances on each node. How many total instances of SQL Server 2000 Enterprise Edition could you place on the cluster and still be supported?

Choose one of the answers below:

1. 1
2. 2
3. 4
4. 8
5. 16
6. 32

Answer:

5. 16

In SQL Server 2000, you can install a total of 16 instances of SQL Server on one machine, whether clustered or on a single stand-alone machine. In a cluster, even though you install SQL Server on machine A it is still installed on any machine participating in the cluster, limitting you to a maximum of 16.

Reference: Microsoft Clustering - http://www.microsoft.com/technet/prodtechnol/sql/2000/maintain/failclus.mspx.

Question 62 - Security

What UDP port does SQL Server listen on?

Choose one of the answers below:

1. 1433
2. 1343
3. 1434
4. 1344
5. None of the above

Answer:

3. 1434

SQL Server's default TCP/IP port is 1433 and uses the UDP port of 1434. You cannot change the UDP port from 1434 to another, which is what helped the SQL Slammer virus spread so quickly. The UDP port is constantly listening on port 1434 and when ping responds with the TCP/IP port SQL Server listens on.

Ref:
http://www.microsoft.com/sql/techinfo/tips/administration/port1434.asp

Question 63 - Security

Mary is a member of a SQL Server user defined role called Accounting. Mary's user has been granted access to the Employees table only in the database but the Accounting role has been revoked access to the table. What is Mary's effective permissions?

Choose one of the answers below:

1. Mary would not be given access to the Employees table.
2. Mary would have access to the Employees table.
3. Mary would only have access to selective data inside the table.
4. Mary would not be able to access the entire database.
5. Mary would be able to read but not update the table.

Answer:

2. Mary would have access to the Employees table.

SQL Server permissions are cummulative. Permissions are also given at the most restrictive. If Mary has been granted access to the table but also revoked access by being a member of the Accounting role, she would be given access to the table. If the Accounting role was denied access to the table, then Mary would not be given access. Revoked access doesn't grant nor deny permissions to an object.

See Revoke.

Question 64 - Security

How would you turn on C2-Level auditing?

Choose one of the answers below:

1. Run the following query:

```
USE master
EXEC sp_configure 'show advanced option', '1'
RECONFIGURE
GO
USE master
EXEC sp_configure 'c2 audit mode', '1'
RECONFIGURE
```

2. Open SQL Profiler, open a new connection and select the C2-Level Audit template.

3. Run the following query:

```
USE master
EXEC sp_configure 'show advanced option', '0'
RECONFIGURE
GO
USE master
EXEC sp_configure 'c2 audit mode', '1'
RECONFIGURE
```

4. Right-click on the server name in SQL Server name in Enterprise Manager and select Properties. Under the Security tab, check C2 Audit Mode.

5. Right-click on the server name in SQL Server name in Enterprise Manager and select Properties. Under the Security tab, check C2-Level Auditing. Finally, stop and start your SQL Server.

Answer:

1. Run the following query:

```
USE master
EXEC sp_configure 'show advanced option', '1'
RECONFIGURE
GO
USE master
EXEC sp_configure 'c2 audit mode', '1'
RECONFIGURE
```

C2-level auditing lets you look at access to any object on a given SQL Server. It does consume a lot of resources while it does do this. It can be enabled by sp_configure. You must first turn on advanced options in sp_configure then turn on the C2-audit.

See C2 Auditing.

Question 65 - Security

You have SQL Server 2000 service pack 3a installed and wish to stop SQL Server from listening on UDP port 1434 and any other UDP port since you application and your database are on the same server. How would you do this?

Choose one of the answers below:

1. Modify the ListenOn DWORD value in the HKEY_LOCAL_MACHINE\SOFTWARE\Microsoft\Microsoft SQL Server registry key.
2. Go to Server Network Utilities and disable all network protocols from the enabled protocols list.
3. Go to Server Network Utilities and select TCP/IP and check Hide Server.
4. Go to Client Network Utilities and disable all network protocols from the enabled protocols list.
5. You can't disable UDP port 1434 in SQL Server.

Answer:

2. Go to Server Network Utilities and disable all network protocols from the enabled protocols list.

In service pack 3a, you can now disable SQL Server from listening on UDP port 1434 by removing all network communications from Server Network Utilities. Previous to this service pack it would still listen on 1434. Now it ceases to respond on the port. This of course will also cease any communication to the server on TCP/IP, which may not be what you want! Again, this would only be the solution if your app and database were on the same server. Ideal for IIS that's installed on the same server or an app hitting a local MSDE instance (for MSDE there's a registry key you'll have to modify).

See How to help secure network connectivity for SQL Server 2000 local databases.

Question 66 - Security

Which one of these common SQL Server network protocols can be configured to support a SQL Server default instance but not a named instance?

Choose one of the answers below:

1. TCP/IP
2. NWLink IPX/SPX
3. Multiprotocol
4. Named Pipes
5. All the above can see a named instance

Answer:

3. Multiprotocol

Of the SQL Server protocols all can see the named instances except for AppleTalk, Banyan Vines, Multiprotocol.

Reference:
Setting Up Client Configuration Entries SQL Server 2000 Books Online, Microsoft Administering SQL Server.
Also Client and Server Net-Libraries

Question 67 - Security

What permissions do you need to run the SELECT @@VERSION query?

Choose one of the answers below:

1. You just need a login into SQL Server.
2. You must have sysadmin rights.
3. You need to have permissions to any database on the server.
4. You need db_datareader rights to the master database.
5. You don't even need a login into SQL Server.

Answer:

1. You just need a login into SQL Server.

To run the query SELECT @@VERSION, which determines the version of SQL Server, you must only have a login into SQL Server.

@@Version.

Question 68 - Security

Which of these steps is not required to turn on C2-Level Auditing?

Choose one of the answers below:

1. Use Enterprise Manager
2. Run the RECONFIGURE statement
3. Use sp_configure
4. Stop and Start SQL Server
5. All the above are required

Answer:

1. Use Enterprise Manager

C2-level auditing mode audits all activity on your SQL Server at a granular level. To enable it, you must run SP_CONFIGURE 'c2 audit mode', 1. Then, type run the RECONFIGURE command and start and stop SQL Server. The command cannot be enabled through the Enterprise Manager GUI.

Question 69 - Security

Where would you find the output of a C2-Level audit for the default instance?

Choose one of the answers below:

1. In the in the \mssql\logs directory for default instances of SQL Server.
2. In the in the \mssql\binn directory for default instances of SQL Server.
3. In the in the \mssql\data directory for default instances of SQL Server.
4. Select from the msdb..sysaudits table.
5. Select from the master..sysaudits table.

Answer:

3. In the in the \mssql\data directory for default instances of SQL Server.

C2-level auditing lets you look at access to any object on a given SQL Server. It does consume a lot of resources while it does do this. Once enabled, C2 auditing tracks C2 audit events and records them to a file in the \mssql\data directory for default instances of SQL Server 2000, or the \mssql$instancename\data directory for named instances of SQL Server 2000.

Reference:Auditing SQL Server.

Question 70 - Security

Due to a new security initiative at Incompetent Inc., C2-level auditing must be enabled on each of your SQL Server 2000 servers. You turn on the option in your production environment with no issues. Two days later however, your SQL Server service on a SQL Server running SQL Server 2000 service pack 1 abruptly stops without explanation. What is the likely cause?

Choose one of the answers below:

1. C2-level auditing has detected that three failed logins have occured on the system in 5 minutes
2. C2-level auditing has detected a malformed SQL query
3. You must install Service Pack 2 for SQL Server 2000
4. Profiler must be on at all times for C2-level auditing to function.
5. The hard drive that holds the C2 logs is full

Answer:

5. The hard drive that holds the C2 logs is full

C2-level auditing writes the SQL Server activity that occurs on the server into a trace and can be up to 250 megabytes for each file. When the drive fills up that holds the trace files, the SQL Server service will stop until space is freed up and the service restarted.

Reference:Auditing SQL Server.

Question 71 - Security

Which is not a way to change your SQL Server login's password?

Choose one of the answers below:

1. By running the following query:

```
UPDATE syslogins
SET password = 'NEWPW'
WHERE login = 'MYLOGIN
```

(substitute the your own values for NEWPW and MYLOGIN.

2. SetPassword Method in DMO

3. The sp_password syntax in T-SQL.

4. Modify the password box in the login properties screen in Enterprise Manager.

Answer:

1. By running the following query:

```
UPDATE syslogins
SET password = 'NEWPW'
WHERE login = 'MYLOGIN
```

(substitute the your own values for NEWPW and MYLOGIN.

Passwords in the syslogins table are encrypted and should not be modified manually.

Question 72 - Security

You are a data security officer for a large corporation. Your database organization has sysadmin access to the SQL Server 2000 server that stores the human resource information. You want to protect a part of the employee table, which holds salary information from the DBAs and do not want them to see a employee_salary column. What is the best way to do this?

Choose one of the answers below:

1. Deny access to the employee_salary column for the DBA logins
2. Revoke access to the employee_salary column for the DBA logins
3. Encrypt the data in the employee_salary column using a 3rd party tool or the application
4. Add the DBA logins to the DENY_DB_READER database role
5. You must do all the above to protect the column

Answer:

3. Encrypt the data in the employee_salary column using a 3rd party tool or the application

If your database organization is in the sysadmin server role, all other column and table permissions are bypassed. WIth that in mind, the only way to make sure that the DBAs can't see the employee_salary column is to encrypt the column on the application side.

Question 73 - Security

Your are a data security specialist for a financial institute and wish to protect certain information for privacy concerns from your application. Because the application that calls the financial data is a fat-client without a middle-tier, all users have direct access to the SQL Server. This makes you worried about a user using Query Analyzer to access certain data directly that the application can't see. If you protect the SocialSecurity column in the Customer table using column-level security in SQL Server, what would happen if the user ran the following query?

```
SELECT * FROM Customer
```

Note: The user has db_datareader and db_datawrite database role rights on the entire database. The user has been denied rights to the SocialSecurity column.

Choose one of the answers below:

1. The user would not see any data
2. The user would see all the columns
3. The user would see only the columns that he has permissions to
4. The social security column would show NULLs and the rest of the data would display

Answer:

1. The user would not see any data

If you ran the above query, the user would receive an error like this: Server: Msg 230, Level 14, State 1, Line 1 SELECT permission denied on column 'SocialSecurity' of object 'Customer', database 'Financial', owner 'dbo'.

This is because the user has been denied rights to a column in the table and tried to see all columns. If the user selected columns other than the SocialSecurity column, he would be able to see the data with no issues.

Question 74 - Security

What is the best way to prevent hackers from exploiting the SQL Server 2000 UDP port running SQL Server 2000 SP2?

Choose one of the answers below:

1. Encrypt communication from that port.
2. Firewall the port
3. Change the UDP port to a more obscure port number
4. Disable the port
5. Turn on Trace Flag 1808

Answer:

2. Firewall the port

SQL Server uses UDP port 1434 as a listener. When pinged it will respond to the pinger with the proper TCP/IP port to communicate out on. It is vulnerable because it may give vital information like this away about your server to a hacker. It should be firewalled to prevent this from occuring. You can turn off the port in SQL Server Service Pack 3 but it is not an easy solution and involves disabling other protocols.

Question 75 - SQL Server Development

You are a database developer for a organization that sells garden gnomes. You are creating a database that will store a history of each order. Orders are entered directly from the customer in an online system. For each new order in the system, a unique order number must be assigned. Order numbers must be assigned in ascending order. On a normal day, 1,000 orders are entered into the system. When creating the order table, you create a OrderID column to store the order number. What is the best thing to do next?

Choose one of the answers below:

1. Set the data type of the OrderID column to int, and set the AUTONUMBER property for the column.
2. Set the data type of the OrderID column to int, and set the IDENTITY property for the column.
3. Set the data type of the OrderID column to uniqueidentifier.
4. Set the data type of the OrderID column to int. Create a user-defined function that selects the maximum order number in the newly created table.
5. Set the data type of the OrderID column to int. Set the column default to SELECT MAX(OrderID) + 1.

Answer:

2. Set the data type of the OrderID column to int, and set the IDENTITY property for the column.

If you set the IDENTITY property on the column, it will automatically increment the value each time a new row is added. The AUTONUMBER property is not a SQL Server property, but an Access one. Setting the column to a uniqueidentifier data type will create a GUID (Global Unique Identiifer) and would not be ascending. The other two options would indeed work, but would create locking problems in your table and would not be the ideal solution.

Question 76 - SQL Server Development

You are a SQL Server developer who wants to get XML quickly out of a database and don't really care about the formatting of the XML. What T-SQL syntax is the fastest way to output default XML in SQL Server 2000 and would be valid.

Choose one of the answers below:

1. SELECT * from tablename with XML
2. SELECT * from tablename for XML
3. SELECT * from tablename with XML AUTO
4. SELECT * from tablename for XML AUTO
5. SELECT * from tablename XML AUTO

Answer:

4. SELECT * from tablename for XML AUTO

The FOR XML AUTO is one of the fastest ways to output XML (although clunky XML) from SQL Server. There are many parameters that can be passed to SQL Server to clean up the formatting of the XML.

See The XML Files.

Question 77 - SQL Server Development

You are a SQL Server developer who's developing a web application that selects against the following table schema:

```
CREATE TABLE SalesData (
SalesID int,
SalesDesc varchar(30),
SalesComments text,
SalesAmmount money)
```

A certain web page in your application runs the following query
*SELECT * FROM SalesData* using ADO. When it retrieves the first record in the loop, the page seems to freeze and no data is displayed other that part of the first row. What is a likely cause?

Choose one of the answers below:

1. Upgrade to the latest version of the IIS
2. Upgrade to the latest version of MDAC
3. Restore from the last known good backup. Your table is probably corrupt.
4. The money data type is not supported in ADO.
5. Rearrange the SELECT statement to where you list the text column last.

Answer:

5. Rearrange the SELECT statement to where you list the text column last.

A common ADO quirk or bug that is actually by design is one that prevents you from seeing the table's text data. To get around this, always arrange your text columns last in your database schema or make sure you select the text fields last in your select statement.

Question 78 - SQL Server Development

You are a SQL Server developer creating a standard ASP form to read from a SQL Server database called Sales on the SQL Server named SalesTracking. You are planning to use the ADO connection object inside your ASP page to connect with an account called SalesUser and a password of PassSales. What would a valid method to connect to SQL Server look like (note: there are many more that are not listed here)?

Choose one of the answers below:

```
1.  Set cn = Server.CreateObject("ADODB.RecordSet")
cn.ConnectionString =
"Driver=SQL;Server;SERVER=SalesTracking;
database=sales;user id=SalesUser;Password=PassSales"
cn.Open
```

```
2. Set cn = Server.CreateObject("ADODB.Connection")
cn.ConnectionString = "Driver=SQL
Server;SERVER=SalesTracking;database=sales;
user id=SalesUser;Password=PassSales"
cn.Open
```

```
3. Set cn = Server.CreateObject("ADODB.Connection")
cn.ConnectionString =
"Driver=MSSQLServer;SOURCE=SalesTracking;database=sale
s;user id=SalesUser;Password=PassSales"
cn.Open
```

```
4. Set cn = Server.CreateObject("ADODB.RecordSet")
cn.ConnectionString =
"Driver=MSSQLServer;SOURCE=SalesTracking;database=sale
s;user id=SalesUser;Password=PassSales"
cn.Open
```

```
5. Set cn = Server.CreateObject("ADODB.Connection")
cn.ConnectionString =
"Driver=MSSQLServer;DSN=SalesTracking;database=sales;
 user id=SalesUser;Password=PassSales"
cn.Open
```

Answer:

2.

```
Set cn = Server.CreateObject("ADODB.Connection")
cn.ConnectionString = "Driver=SQL
Server;SERVER=SalesTracking;database=sales;
                              user
id=SalesUser;Password=PassSales"
cn.Open
```

The connection object in ADO can be managed with three lines of code. shown here:


```
Set cn = Server.CreateObject("ADODB.Connection")
cn.ConnectionString = "Driver=SQL
Server;SERVER=SalesTracking;database=sales;
                              user
id=SalesUser;Password=PassSales"
cn.Open
```

Question 79 - SQL Server Development

You are a SQL Server developer who is trying to create an indexed view on several tables. Which of the following is <u>not</u> a requirement when you create an indexed view?

Choose one of the answers below:

1. The view can't reference any other views.
2. The view must be created with the SCHEMABINDING option
3. All functions referenced by the view must be deterministic
4. The ANSI_NULLS nulls option must have been set to ON when you created the tables using the CREATE TABLE syntax.
5. You must use the three-part name to reference the tables (databasename.owner.table)

Answer:

5. You must use the three-part name to reference the tables (databasename.owner.table)

There are quite a few requirements for indexed views. Among other things, indexed views must use two-part names (owner.table) inside the view for all queries.

Reference: Creating an Indexed View in Books Online

Also Indexed Views.

Question 80 - SQL Server Development

You are a SQL Server developer who is attempting to create a view called vArticles via T-SQL that selects all records from the Articles table and orders the results by their creation date from the oldest article to the newest article. You use the following query to create the view:

```
CREATE VIEW vArticles as
SELECT *
 FROM Articles
 ORDER BY CreateDt
```

but it fails with the following error (some piece of the error left out to save room):

```
Server: Msg 1033, Level 15, State 1, Procedure
vArticles, Line 4
The ORDER BY clause is invalid in views, inline
functions, derived tables, and ubqueries...
```

How would you fix the T-SQL to make the view create and return the desired effect?

Choose one of the answers below:

```
1. CREATE VIEW vArticles as
SELECT TOP 100 * FROM Articles
ORDER BY CreateDt
```

```
2. CREATE VIEW vArticles as
SELECT * FROM Articles
ORDER BY CreateDt DESC
```

```
3. CREATE VIEW vArticles as
SELECT * FROM Articles
ORDER BY CreateDt ASC
```

```
4. CREATE VIEW vArticles as
SELECT TOP 100 PERCENT * FROM Articles
ORDER BY CreateDt
```

```
5. CREATE VIEW vArticles as
SELECT * FROM dbo.Articles
ORDER BY CreateDt
```

Answer:

4.

```
CREATE VIEW
vArticles as
SELECT TOP 100 PERCENT * FROM Articles
ORDER BY CreateDt
```

The workaround is to add the top clause in the query as is shown in the answer. You can add any top clause like TOP 100 but TOP 100 PERCENT would return the desired effect, as it returns the entire table of records.

Behavior of the ORDER BY clause in views, derived tables, inline functions, and subqueries in SQL 2000.

Question 81 - SQL Server Development

You are a database designer and you see a column with the following data type:
decimal (5,3)
What type of number would be properly represented by the above data type and data without rounding (for example, the value in the answer must not be rounded once you try to select from the table)?

Choose one of the answers below:

1. 11.111
2. 111.11
3. 1.1111
4. 11111
5. .11111

Answer:

1. 11.111

Numeric and decimal data types use precision and scale to represent a numeric value as shown below:
decimal[(p[, s])] and numeric[(p[, s])]
p (precision) - Specifies the maximum total number of decimal digits that can be stored, both to the left and to the right of the decimal point. The precision must be a value from 1 through the maximum precision. The maximum precision is 38. The default precision is 18.
s (scale) - Specifies the maximum number of decimal digits that can be stored to the right of the decimal point. Scale must be a value from 0 through p. Scale can be specified only if precision is specified. The default scale is 0; therefore, 0 <= s <= p. Maximum storage sizes vary, based on the precision.

Question 82 - SQL Server Development

You are a database developer and you want to log who makes a change to the database. Users log in to the application using their own SQL logins. For example, when a user logs in with the login sa and inserts a record, you wish to log that this was done by the sa login. You decide the best way to do this is by adding a column into a table that holds who added the record and change the DEFAULT attribute to use the system function for this. What system function would ouptut the login of the user who's performing an action. For example, you login with bknight, bknight would be inserted into the column with the default attrbiute.

Choose one of the answers below:

1. login_name
2. user
3. system_user
4. session_user
5. user_name()

Answer:

3. system_user

The system_user function can be used to determine what login the user signed in with. For example, to call the function use the following syntax:

```
SELECT SYSTEM_USER
```

Question 83 - SQL Server Development

You are a database developer who is trying to perform a query against a datetime column in a table with accounting records. You want all entries for a specific date, August 1st 2003, regardless of the time on the day. Which of the below methods would satisfy that requirement? (Note: The dots (...) represent the FROM TABLENAME statement.)
Contributed by Kay-Ole Behrmann

Choose one of the answers below:

1. SELECT .... WHERE CONVERT(varchar, DateVal, 101) = '08/01/2003'
2. SELECT .... WHERE DateVal BETWEEN '2003-08-01' AND '2003-08-01 23:59:59.997'
3. SELECT .... WHERE DateVal >= '2003-08-01' AND DateVal < '2003-08-02'
4. SELECT .... WHERE CAST(FLOOR(CAST(DateVal AS float))AS datetime)='8/1/2003'
5. All of the above
6. None of the above

Answer:

5. All of the above

The first solution converts to varchar format "101", i.e. US-Format mm/dd/yyyy, and compares to a string. Doing it this way however, chances are you forget leading zeros (8/1/2003) and get no results. The second solution uses knowledge about the largest possible timepart in a datetime, wich is not a particularly pretty way. The third way is the classic one, using two date-only values with an implicit time of 00:00:00.0000 and forces a "greater or equal" to midnight 8/1 and a "less than" midnight 8/2. Answer #4 cuts off the time part of the datetime value by removing decimals from the converted float-value. This makes use of the fact that conversion to a float stores the date in the integer-part and time in the decimals.

Question 84 - SQL Server Development

Which of the following data types cannot be used as a parameter in a Stored Procedure with SQL Server 2000? Contributed by James Travis

Choose one of the answers below:

1. text
2. table
3. cursor
4. sql_variant

Answer:

2. table

All data types, except the table data type, can be used as a parameter for a stored procedure. However, the cursor data type can be used only on OUTPUT parameters. When you specify a data type of cursor, the VARYING and OUTPUT keywords must also be specified. Reference : Books Online - CREATE PROCEDURE.

Question 85 - SQL Server Development

You have developed a bulk insert process using to load 100,000 records into a SQL Server 2000 table. The process will use the BULK INSERT T-sQL command that is shown below to load the records.

```
BULK INSERT Inventory.dbo.Orders
   FROM 'c:\orders\lineitem.tbl'
   WITH
      (
         FIELDTERMINATOR = '|',
         ROWTERMINATOR = '|\n'
      )
```

The table has an INSERT trigger and INSTEAD OF trigger on it. What would be the behavior of the triggers during the load?

Choose one of the answers below:

1. Only the INSERT trigger would be executed
2. Only the INSTEAD OF trigger would execute
3. Both triggers would execute
4. None of the triggers would execute

Answer:

4. None of the triggers would execute

Neither one of the triggers would fire. In SQL Server 2000 the BULK INSERT command bulk loads data and by default would not use triggers. To use triggers you can add the FIRE_TRIGGERS BULK INSERT hint, which woud direct the triggers to fire after all the rows have been inserted. Referance: Bulk Insert.

Question 86 - SQL Server Development

What is the most number of bytes that any type of integer data type can be in SQL Server 2000?

Choose one of the answers below:

1. 1
2. 2
3. 4
4. 8
5. 16

Answer:

4. 8

SQL Server 2000 offers support of integer values up to 8 bytes with the new bigint data type. This can store whole numbers from –2^63 (-9,223,372,036,854,775,808) through 2^63-1 (9,223,372,036,854,775,807). In previous releases of SQL Server, the largest integer data type was an integer of 4 bytes. Reference: Choosing SQL Server 2000 Datatypes.

Question 87 - SQL Server Development

You are taking over for another DBA and are trying to audit some of his scripts. You sign in with the login of bknight and execute the following script. Given the script below, what would be the result of its execution?

```
CREATE TABLE DEMO
(Primary int,
Name varchar(30) DEFAULT SYSTEM_USER)

GO
INSERT DEMO (Primary) VALUES(1)
SELECT * FROM DEMO
```

Choose one of the answers below:

1. The values of 1 and bknight
2. The values of 1 and dbo
3. The values of 1 and NULL
4. The values of bknight and 1
5. An error

Answer:

5. An error

The script would error on the table creation because the column name of Primary is a reserved word. If the script were to execute properly though, you would receive the results of 1 and bknight as the SYSTEM_USER function returns the login that you're signed in with.

Question 88 - SQL Server Development

You are a SQL Server developer who is trying to retrieve a rate description from a varchar(3000) column called RatesDescription in a table called Rates. You want to retrieve any records that mention a rate of 5% in the description but the following query is not working:

```
select * from rates where
RateDescription like '%5%'
```

Retrieves more records than you need (note the 5PM):

RateDescription
~~~~~~
Rate of 5% is effective until 5PM on Friday
Rate of 2% is effective until 5PM on Monday
Rate of 4% is effective until 5PM on Tuesday

How would you fix the query to retrieve the appropriate results (only one record)?

Choose one of the answers below:

1. SET QUOTED_IDENTIFIER OFF GO select * from rates where RateDescription like "%5%"
2. select * from rates where RateDescription like '%5%%'

3. select * from rates where RateDescription like '%5/%' ESCAPE '/'
4. select * from rates where RateDescription like '%5/% %' ESCAPE '/'
5. None of the above
~~~~~~

Answer:

4. select * from rates where RateDescription like '%5/%%' ESCAPE '/'

Use the ESCAPE keyword to define an escape character. When the escape character is placed in front of the wildcard in the pattern, the wildcard is interpreted as a character. For example, to search for the string 5% anywhere in a string, use: WHERE ColumnA LIKE '%5/%%' ESCAPE '/'. In this LIKE clause, the leading and ending percent signs (%) are interpreted as wildcards, and the percent sign preceded by a slash (/) is interpreted as the % character.

Reference Books Online: Pattern Matching in Search Conditions.

Question 89 - SQL Server Development

John is a SQL Server developer who is writing T-SQL to loop through a set of results in perform an action in a set of cursor. The users who execute the query will have SELECT and INSERT rights in the table. What must he worry about when using the @@FETCH_STATUS function in his code?

Choose one of the answers below:

1. The @@FETCH_STATUS function can only be used by sysadmins.
2. The @@FETCH_STATUS function is shared across all cursors in all connections.
3. The @@FETCH_STATUS function is shared across all cursors in a connection.
4. The @@FETCH_STATUS function also requires that the user have UPDATE rights to the table
5. The @@FETCH_STATUS function will always return an error.

Answer:

3. The @@FETCH_STATUS function is shared across all cursors in a connection.

The @@FETCH_STATUS scalar function returns the status of the last cursor FETCH statement issued against any cursor currently opened by the connection. Because @@FETCH_STATUS is global to all cursors on a connection, use @@FETCH_STATUS carefully. After a FETCH statement is executed, the test for @@FETCH_STATUS must occur before any other FETCH statement is executed against another cursor.

Reference:
@@Fetch_status.

Question 90 - SQL Server Development

You are a SQL Server developer who is attempting to use data link files (UDL files) to connect to a SQL Server. What is the largest consideration or worry for you to keep in mind when using UDL files and shipping them to clients?

Reference: Handling Package Security in DTS.

Choose one of the answers below:

1. UDL files are always cached at design time and can't be changed after the application is compiled
2. You won't be able to use them in an unattended process like a job since UDL files prompt for a password
3. UDL files require that you have at least MDAC 2.6 to properly connect to SQL Server
4. UDL are unencrypted files
5. UDL files don't work on SQL Server 7.0 and before

Answer:

4. UDL are unencrypted files

The largest concern with UDL files is the security risk of passing unencrypted files between users. Everything, including the password can possibly be unencrypted. Use Windows Authentication for the connection. Windows Authentication does not require login information to be placed in the data link file. It only requires a flag indicating that a trusted connection will be used. This connection method is secure for data link files. Sometimes, UDL files will be cached at design time but there are configuration options that can be set to override that problem.

Reference : Books Online "Handling Package Security in DTS"

Question 91 - SQL Server Development

You are a SQL Server 2000 developer who is trying to use Index Tuning Wizard for the first time to add indexes to a table with 50 columns in the table. The results the tool returns though suggests that Index Tuning Wizard wants to create an index on 16 columns for one index. You wish to limit the amount of columns per index and rerun the wizard. How could you accomplish this goal?

Choose one of the answers below:

1. In the wizard, set the Tuning Mode to Medium in the Select Server and Database screen.
2. In the wizard, set the Maximum Columns Per Index option in the Specify Workload screen.
3. In the wizard, set the Maximum Columns Per Index option in the Advanced Options screen under the Specify Workload screen.
4. Set the Maximum Columns Per Index option under Tools | Options in the Index Tuning Wizard
5. In the registry of the computer running Index Tuning Wizard, edit the MaxColumns DWORD in the HKEY_LOCAL_MACHINE\SOFTWARE\Microsoft\Microsoft SQL Server\80\Tools\Profiler key.

Answer:

3. In the wizard, set the Maximum Columns Per Index option in the Advanced Options screen under the Specify Workload screen.

A common issue that you may experience with the Index Tuning Wizard is that it may too agressivily add too many columns in an index. To limit this, in the wizard set the Maximum Columns Per Index option in the Advanced Options screen under the Specify Workload screen.

Question 92 - SQL Server Development

You create a table called [member] as part of a database. After building some of the rest of the database and addind 24 rows to the [member] table you check out the sysindexes table and you notice the following two rows relating to this [member] table:

```
select i.indid, i.FirstIAM, i.dpages, i.[rows],
i.rowmodctr, i.[name]
from sysindexes i
join sysobjects o on i.[id] = o.[id] where o.
[name] = N'member'

indid  FirstIAM       dpages      rows
rowmodctr   name
------ -------------- ----------- -----------
------------------------------------
0      0x800200000100 1           24
24         member
2      0x000000000000 0           0
-24        _WA_Sys_lastname_5031C87B
```

Which of the following could be true about the [member] table?

Provided by Keith Henry

Choose one of the answers below:

1. It has a text field called lastname.
2. The data is in a heap with a system index called _WA_Sys_lastname_5031C87B
3. The data is in a heap and auto_create_statistics is on
4. The data has a non-clustered index called _WA_Sys_lastname_5031C87B
5. The index on this table was created with Enterprise Manager on the field [lastname]

Answer:

3. The data is in a heap and auto_create_statistics is on

The first row with indid of zero indicates that the data is in a heap with the first IAM at 0x800200000100
If there was a text field in the table it would have a row in sysindexes with indid 255
If _WA_Sys_lastname_5031C87B was an index it would have a FirstIAM value other than 0x000000000000
SQL server stores statistics in the sysindexes table in a format similar to non-clustered indexes (they even use indid 2-250) however the FirstIAM does not point to the start of the index.
If auto_create_statistics is on for a database SQL server will generate statisics with the format: _WA_Sys__

Question 93 - SQL Server Development

What would be the results of executing the following query against a SQL Server 7.0 database server?

```
SET NOCOUNT ON
declare @last_status table
          (run_status int,
          run_date int,
          run_time int)

insert @last_status
          select top 1 run_status, max
(run_date), max(run_time)
          from msdb..sysjobhistory
          where job_id = '1617076F-2DD8-4CFC-
8ED2-28F2FE4E1BE7'
          and step_name = '(Job outcome)'
          GROUP BY run_status
          ORDER BY 2 desc, 3 desc

select * from @last_status
```

(Note: the job_id GUID shown in the where clause will change based on the job you wish to query)

Choose one of the answers below:

1. You would retrieve the run status, date and time of the job that matches the GUID.
2. An error would be received because he table data type does not exist in SQL Server 7.0
3. The sysjobhistory table does not exist in SQL Server 2000
4. The ORDER BY clause would output an error
5. The GROUP BY clause would output an error
6. You cannot use the MAX() function against a datetime column.

Answer:

2. An error would be received because he table data type does not exist in SQL Server 7.0

The table data type was first introduced in SQL Server 2000 and would generate an error if you tried to run the script. If you ran the script in SQL Server 2000, you would retrieve the run status, date and time of the job that matches the GUID.

Question 94 - SQL Server Development

What would the following statement output in Query Analyzer?

```
BEGIN TRAN
SET NOCOUNT ON
UPDATE authors SET au_lname = 'White'
WHERE au_id = '213-46-8915'
ROLLBACK
PRINT @@ROWCOUNT
```

Choose one of the answers below:

1. An error
2. The number of rows that were affected by the UPDATE statement before it rolls back
3. The number of rows that were not affected by the UPDATE statement before it rolls back
4. Number of rows in the table
5. The number 0

Answer:

5. The number 0

The above statement would update the authors table in the pubs database. But before it actually comits the data, would rollback the statement, thereby actually not updating any records. The @@ROWCOUNT function outputs the number of rows affected by the statement and since there are no records updated, it would output 0.

Question 95 - SQL Server Development

What statement is <u>not</u> true about timestamp columns.

Choose one of the answers below:

1. A table can have only one timestamp column.
2. The value in the timestamp column is updated every time a row containing a timestamp column is inserted or updated
3. They make excellent choices for Primary Keys since they're guaranteed to be unique
4. They automatically generate binary numbers, which are guaranteed to be unique within a database.
5. All the above are correct

Answer:

3. They make excellent choices for Primary Keys since they're guaranteed to be unique

Timestamp is a data type that exposes automatically generated binary numbers, which are guaranteed to be unique within a database. timestamp is used typically as a mechanism for version-stamping table rows. The storage size is 8 bytes. A table can have only one timestamp column. The value in the timestamp column is updated every time a row containing a timestamp column is inserted or updated. This property makes a timestamp column a poor candidate for keys, especially primary keys. Any update made to the row changes the timestamp value, thereby changing the key value. If the column is in a primary key, the old key value is no longer valid, and foreign keys referencing the old value are no longer valid. If the table is referenced in a dynamic cursor, all updates change the position of the rows in the cursor. If the column is in an index key, all updates to the data row also generate updates of the index.

Reference: timestamp datatype - http://msdn.microsoft.com/library/default.asp?url=/library/en-us/tsqlref/ts_ta-tz_6fn4.asp.

Question 96 - SQL Server Development

You have a table with the following schema:

```
CREATE TABLE Customers(
PrimaryName varchar(30),
LastUpdate timestamp)
```

Records are inserted and updated into this table on a regular basis and the timestamp is updated every time a change is made on the row or when when a row is inserted. You want to determine when the customer named Brian (in the PrimaryName column) was last updated from the LastUpdate column in a format like this "2003-10-12 10:03:39.123". How could you achieve this?

Choose one of the answers below:

1. SELECT LastUpdate FROM Customers WHERE PrimaryName = 'Brian'
2. SELECT CONVERT(datetime,LastUpdate) FROM Customers WHERE PrimaryName = 'Brian'
3. SELECT CAST(LastUpdate AS datetime) FROM Customers WHERE PrimaryName = 'Brian'
4. SELECT CONVERT(varchar(10),LastUpdate) FROM Customers WHERE PrimaryName = 'Brian'
5. SELECT CAST(LastUpdate AS varchar(10)) FROM Customers WHERE PrimaryName = 'Brian'
6. The objective can't be met with a timestamp column

Answer:

6. The objective can't be met with a timestamp column

timestamp is a data type that exposes automatically generated binary numbers, which are guaranteed to be unique within a database. timestamp is used typically as a mechanism for version-stamping table rows. The storage size is 8 bytes. The Transact-SQL timestamp data type is not the same as the timestamp data type defined in the SQL-92 standard. The SQL-92 timestamp data type is equivalent to the Transact-SQL datetime data type. If you tried to convert this timestamp column to a datetime or varchar column, the result would be something like this: 1900-01-01 00:00:00.670 and not provide you the desired results. So, no conversion or direct viewing would provide anything close to what you're trying to achieve.

Reference: timestamp datatype - http://msdn.microsoft.com/library/default.asp?url=/library/en-us/tsqlref/ts_ta-tz_6fn4.asp.

Question 97 - SQL Server Development

A programmer is attempting to select rows entered today from a table in the database. What's a common reason that this query:

```
select * from table where datefield = getdate()
```

would return no records or far fewer than were expected? Assume that datefield is really declared as a datetime and that some records really have today's date.

Contributed by Darwin Hatheway

Choose one of the answers below:

1. GETDATE() cannot be compared directly to a column, you must use a local variable with the current GETDATE () in it.
2. The precision returned by GETDATE() is incompatible with the precision of date times stored in the database. You must use the CONVERT function as a bridge.
3. The value to be returned by GETDATE() is set when your session is created or, if using a stored procedure, when the stored procedure is compiled and comparisons with GETDATE() can have unpredictable results for this reason.
4. The call to GETDATE() will return both the date and the current time, which very likely not match the data in the datefield, whether the date only was stored or both the date and time were stored..
5. The collation setting of your database needs to be adjusted to match the national settings of your client.

Answer:

4. The call to GETDATE() will return both the date and the current time, which very likely not match the data in the datefield, whether the date only was stored or both the date and time were stored..

The call to GETDATE() will return both the date and the current time, which very likely not match the data in the datefield, whether the date only was stored or both the date and time were stored.. The worst case is where both the date and time are stored in the field and only the date is really of interest. It will then be very difficult to query this table by date without using range searches or a function that converts the date and time on every row to just a date.

Question 98 - SQL Server Development

Which of the following statements is true?

Choose one of the answers below:

1. SQL Server 2000 supports two methods of indexing, B-Tree and Hash and applies the appropriate type automatically.
2. Creating an index will block a BACKUP operation.
3. When creating a clustered index, you can dramatically decrease the amount of work space required in the user database by using the WITH SORT_IN_TEMPDB option.

4. With SQL Server 2000, your index columns may now total about 8K bytes in width, like the data columns themselves.
5. Statements 1-4 are all false.

Answer:

5. Statements 1-4 are all false.

Not true. Only B-Trees are supported by MS. You might have been thinking of clustered vs non-clustered as two types of indexing and that would have been true.
Not true. If necessary, indexing will be done in a fully-logged mode, compatible with BACKUP.
Not true. Although TEMPDB can now be used for intermediate sort runs - and may improve index creation performance and contiguity - the amount of work space required in the user database will still be equal to the size of the original table and the new table copy.
Not true. You run into trouble with indexes at 900 bytes, depending on fixed and variable field widths.

Question 99 - SQL Server Development

A programmer calls you over to his desk with a query problem on a stored procedure you wrote. What is the error in this situation? The table is declared as: mytable (mykey int, myfield varchar(255)). This procedure

```
create procedure myproc
@a_key   int, @a_field    varchar(40)
as
update mytable set myfield = @a_field where mykey =
@a_key
if (@@error <> 0)          return -1
if @@rowcount = 0          return 0
return 1
```

is used by our programmer this way:

```
declare @retval int
exec @retval = myproc 1, 'first rec'
select case  @retval
      when  0 then 'no rows updated'
      when  -1 then 'error encountered'
      else  'update complete'
      end
```

Choose one of the answers below:

1. IF statements require BEGIN and END keywords.
2. Your return values must be declared in the header.
3. The mykey field in mytable is not declared as a primary key or unique constraint and can't be used for the constraint in the update statement.
4. The 'end procedure' statement is missing.
5. The 'not equal' test must be "@@error != 0"
6. The 'if @@rowcount = 0' test is not meaningful and the "no rows updated" message will always display.
7. "@@rowcount = 0" must be enclosed in parentheses.

Answer:

6. The 'if @@rowcount = 0' test is not meaningful and the "no rows updated" message will always display.

The @@ROWCOUNT variable will be reset by the IF statement that followed the UPDATE and won't be meaningful for the IF @@rowcount = 0 test, so the 'no rows updated message will always be displayed, whether any rows were updated or not.

Contributed by Darwin Hatheway

Question 100 - SQL Server Development

Jon signs in to the development server with the login of DeveloperAcct to create a new stored procedure called usp_callrec. Jon is not a sysadmin and is not a database owner but has adaquate permissions to create the procedure. The development server is SQL Server 2000 Service Pack 1. The other developers try to access the usp_callrec stored procedure by name but keep receiving an error "Could Not Find Stored Procedure". Jon can access the stored procedure without any issues. What is the most likely problem?

Choose one of the answers below:

1. The developers will need to use the name developeracct.usp_callrec to access the stored procdure.

2. The developers will need to use the name dbo.usp_callrec to access the stored procdure.
3. Jon must be a sysadmin for others to use the stored procedure
4. Jon must be a database owner for others to use the stored procedure
5. You must be on Service Pack 2 or later of SQL Server 2000

Answer:

1. The developers will need to use the name developeracct.usp_callrec to access the stored procdure.

If you are not the dbo of the database, the stored procedure will be named based on your account's name. So Jon's stored procedure would be named DeveloperAcct.uspcallrec instead of just uspcallrec.